MW01279919

Treasure
and
Owl and Pussy

Hannie Truijens

Nelson

Treasure

Meg was in her attic.
She looked in the old box.
"What is this?" she said.

"It is a treasure map," said Ben.
"Let's go and look for the
treasure," said Sam.

The friends got a boat and
went out to sea.
They rowed and rowed.
"It is too hot to row," said Jip.

4

Ben looked at the map.

"We must dig here," he said.

The friends dug and dug.

"It is too hot to dig," said Deb.

Deb looked at the map again.

"Look," she said.

"It is not this tree.

We must dig next to that tree."

The friends dug and dug.

"It is too hot to dig," said Meg.

At last they found the treasure.

The friends put the treasure
in the boat and went out to sea.
They rowed and rowed.
"It is too hot to row," said Sam.

The treasure fell into the sea.
The friends had to swim home.
"It isn't too hot to swim,"
said Ben.

9

The friends were home at last.
"We found the treasure," they said.
"But we lost it again."

Owl and Pussy

Owl said to Pussy,
"I like you, I do."
And Pussy cat said,
"My dear, I do too."

"Let's go, my sweet Owl.
Let's go out to sea.
We can go and come back.
What a game it will be.

Dear Owl and sweet Pussy
then got a tall tree
and made a small boat
to go out to sea.

The wind blew so strong
it blew them away.
They sat on that sea
for all of a day.

Out came the moon,
away went the sun.
Sweet Owl and dear Pussy
ate cake and a bun.

Strong grew the wind
and cold grew the sky.
"Let's go now," said Pussy
and home they did fly.

treasure

MW01280267

SOCIAL SCIENCE

Pirates:
Robbers at Sea

MICHÈLE DUFRESNE

TABLE OF CONTENTS

sland

ATTACK ON THE HIGH SEAS

In 1717, a large French slave ship named *La Concorde* was crossing the Atlantic Ocean. The ship had traveled for months from France to Africa and was not well armed. It had gunports for 40 cannons, but most were empty in order to make room for cargo and the 516 slaves chained below deck.

Suddenly, two fast sloops appeared on the horizon. They quickly caught up to the slave ship, then raised a pirate flag and fired two rounds of shots over the bow. Unable to fight or outrun the pirate ships, the French captain quickly surrendered.

Piracy means robbery at sea.

The pirate captain was Edward Teach, but he was better known as Blackbeard. He had started out as a sailor on a ship that worked for the British government. It attacked and **plundered** French and Spanish ships because Britain was fighting against those nations. When the war was over, Edward became a pirate captain.

Blackbeard and his crew brought the French ship to shore and unloaded its food and valuables. They kept some of the slaves, who are believed to have joined the pirate crew. Blackbeard also kept *La Concorde* and renamed it *Queen Anne's Revenge*.

Blackbeard was known for his ferocious appearance, especially an enormous black beard braided with ribbons.

DANGEROUS WATERS

Pirates have roamed the oceans for as long as ships have sailed the seas. As merchant ships carried gold, jewels, and goods from place to place, they had to follow routes that had good winds and currents and places to stop for fresh drinking water.

MORE TO EXPLORE

Greek and Roman pirates robbed **TRADING SHIPS** and seized passengers thousands of years ago in the Mediterranean Sea.

Certain areas became notorious for piracy. Pirates lay waiting along these routes, ready to plunder the treasure-filled ships.

The island of Madagascar was used by pirates as a base for operations in the Indian Ocean.

The Caribbean Sea was a very popular raiding ground for pirates and **buccaneers**.

The **corsairs** of the Barbary Coast plundered ships in the Mediterranean Sea.

Pirates hunted merchant ships in the South China Sea.

After the discovery of the New World and trade routes to India, piracy became much more popular. Between 1650 and 1720, thousands of pirates targeted ships transporting goods to Europe. They also launched attacks on New World coastal towns.

MORE TO EXPLORE

Pirates often **FREED AFRICAN SLAVES** and recruited them into their crew. These new pirates received shares of treasure and voted with the crew on important matters.

Speed was important for successful piracy. It allowed pirates to catch up to slow-moving merchant vessels. Speed also allowed pirates to escape their enemies with stolen treasure and other goods. Sometimes, to look friendly, a pirate ship would fly a false flag and cover its gunports. When it got close enough to fire, the pirates would raise their true flag. Some pirate captains would fire a couple of warning shots to encourage surrender without damaging the ship itself. It was always better to capture a ship and its crew without bloodshed.

The pirate flag was commonly referred to as the Jolly Roger.

If the ship's crew decided to fight back, the pirates would use grappling hooks to pull the two ships together, then attempt to shoot the captain and officers and board the ship. They battled the crew with swords, pistols, muskets, and other weapons.

Sometimes useful crew members from the captured ship would be **press-ganged** into service on the pirate vessel. A carpenter was highly valued because he could help keep a boat afloat.

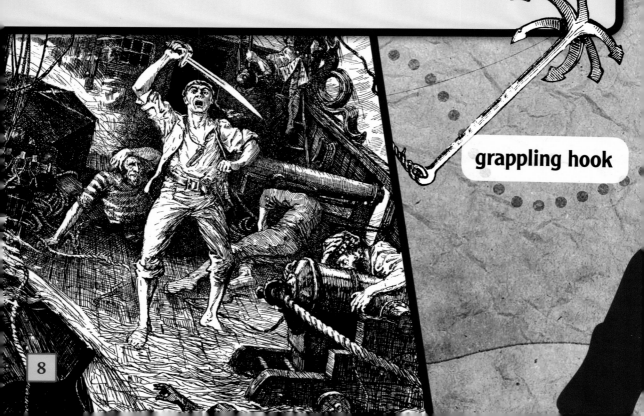

grappling hook

Once a ship was theirs, the pirates might add it to their fleet if it was in good condition. Sometimes they needed the ship to carry stolen cargo back to port to sell. Some captured ships were sold. Others were set adrift or sunk if they were not worth anything.

MORE TO EXPLORE

Did pirates make captives **WALK THE PLANK?** Probably not. They more likely flogged their victims or simply threw them overboard.

A PIRATE'S LIFE FOR ME

Life aboard a pirate ship could be hard and dangerous. Bad storms, spoiled food, foul water, and injuries from battles were common. Pirates lived in filthy, cramped quarters, and **stowaway** rats were often their roommates. But crew members had more freedom and rights than sailors on merchant vessels. Pirate ships were usually run **democratically**, so the crew chose their own captain. If pirates thought their captain was too harsh or making bad decisions, they could remove the captain and vote in a new one.

When a pirate lost an eye in battle, they wore an eye patch to cover the damage.

A pirate's activities at sea were much like any sailor's. They played cards and dice. They made wood carvings, sang, and danced jigs. They took care of the ship, keeping it watertight and its sails free of holes.

There are many stories about pirates burying their treasure. But after a raid, pirates divided up their booty and sailed into a friendly port, where they spent their ill-gotten gains. Ashore, they often dressed like gentlemen in fancy coats and shoes with heels and silver buckles.

MORE TO EXPLORE

Some pirates wore earrings because they believed they **PREVENTED SEASICKNESS** by putting pressure on the earlobes.

PRIVATEERING

While most pirates simply were in search of riches, others were privateers, encouraged by governments to attack and raid enemy ships. During the American Revolution, the 13 colonies had very few sailors or ships. To combat the mighty British navy, privately owned ships were permitted to attack, **subdue**, and take ships belonging to the British.

Strict rules had to be followed. Privateers were not allowed to abuse officers and crew or hold them for ransom. Instead, prisoners were turned over to officials on land. Just like regular pirates, privateers divided the **swag**. Half the haul went to the ship's owner, and the rest was divided among the captain and crew.

FAMOUS PIRATES AND PRIVATEERS

Many stories, movies, plays, books, and songs portray pirates as romantic heroes, but in fact, most pirates lived rough, murderous lives. If they were captured, they were put to death for their deeds.

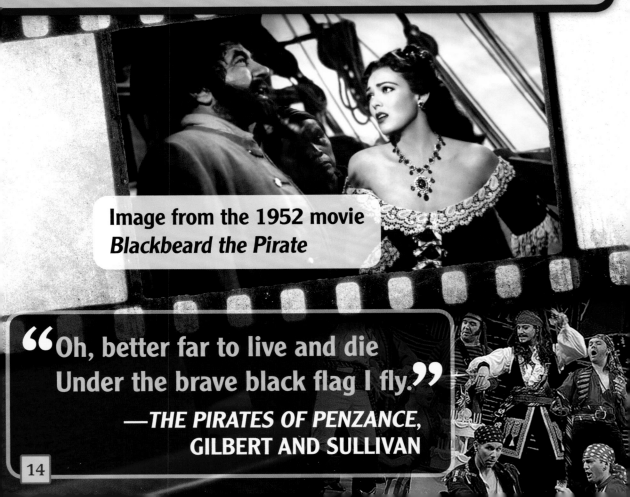

Image from the 1952 movie
Blackbeard the Pirate

66Oh, better far to live and die
Under the brave black flag I fly.**99**

—*THE PIRATES OF PENZANCE,*
GILBERT AND SULLIVAN

William Kidd, 1645–1701

William Kidd began his career as a privateer hired to attack foreign ships. Then he found himself on the wrong side of the law after he and his crew attacked a large merchant ship in the Indian Ocean. It was owned by a man with powerful connections and carried gold, spices, silk, and other goods.

After a trial, William was hanged in London. To serve as a warning to other pirates, his body was left to rot in public. Some wonder what happened to Captain Kidd's treasure. Is it buried somewhere, still waiting for someone to discover it?

Samuel Bellamy, 1689–1717

Captain Samuel Bellamy and his crew raided at least 53 ships. Samuel was known for mercy toward those he captured. Some called him the "Prince of Pirates," and his crew called themselves "Robin Hood's Men." Samuel's piracy was very short-lived. After a little over a year, he and most of his crew died in a shipwreck when their vessel, the *Whydah*, sank off the coast of Massachusetts.

For many years, treasure hunters searched for the *Whydah*, wondering just how much treasure was buried inside. Then underwater explorer Barry Clifford found the ship's remains in 1984. Barry and his team recovered the *Whydah*'s treasure as well as many interesting artifacts.

Samuel Bellamy

Anne Bonny, 1700–1782

Not all pirates were men. Anne Bonny married a sailor, but it was an unhappy marriage. She left her husband to join the crew of pirate John "Calico Jack" Rackham. She was not the only woman pirate on the ship. Later, Mary Read also joined the crew. When the ship attacked others, both women dressed like men and fought side by side with the male pirates.

The crew embarked on daring raids of Spanish treasure ships near Cuba and Hispaniola. During a raid along the north coast of Jamaica, their ship was captured. John and the crew were sentenced to hang, but Anne and Mary were spared because they were both pregnant.

Anne Bonny

Calico Jack

17

PIRACY TODAY

Pirates are not just part of the past. They still terrorize the seas in different parts of the world, and many countries do not have water police or anyone able to stop them. Pirates now travel in high-speed boats and carry machine guns and rocket-propelled grenade launchers. They use modern technology to locate ships and communicate with other criminals on shore.

MORE TO EXPLORE

Today's pirates often pursue **SMALLER CARGO SHIPS.** Because those vessels have to slow down to move through narrow passages, they are simpler to attack than larger ones.

But modern pirates have many things in common with ones from long ago. They hide their flags and disguise themselves as government ships. They kidnap people for ransom, and they rob and murder people. Because piracy scares shipowners away from some areas, the economies of nearby countries suffer as well.

MORE TO EXPLORE

In 2005, pirates **KEPT RICE** from reaching poor people in Africa. The stolen rice would have fed 28,000 of Somalia's tsunami victims for at least two months.

Pirate Sayings

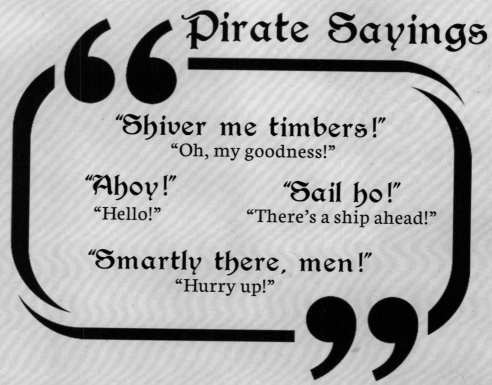

"Shiver me timbers!"
"Oh, my goodness!"

"Ahoy!"
"Hello!"

"Sail ho!"
"There's a ship ahead!"

"Smartly there, men!"
"Hurry up!"

A Pirate's Life

Most pirate ships carried a huge number of four-legged stowaways: rats! All those rats onboard caused a number of problems, as they would eat the pirates' food, chew their ropes, and spread diseases.

Did you know that many pirates suffered from a disease called scurvy, which causes fatigue and pain? Today we know that scurvy can be prevented when you eat enough vitamin C. Pirates could have easily prevented it by including fruit and vegetables in their provisions.

Pirate Facts

Ever wonder what a pirate's life was really like? Not as wild as you might expect. In fact, they had rules for everything, from how to fight like a pirate to sharing loot. These strict rules were known as the pirate code.

Parts of a Pirate Ship

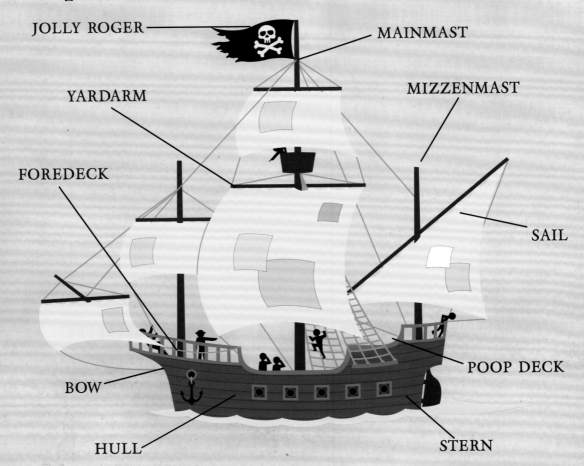

JOLLY ROGER

MAINMAST

YARDARM

MIZZENMAST

FOREDECK

SAIL

BOW

POOP DECK

HULL

STERN

GLOSSARY

buccaneers
pirates who operated around some
of the islands in the Caribbean Sea

corsairs
pirates who operated in
the Mediterranean Sea

democratically
selected by a vote of the people

plundered
stole something by force

press-ganged
forced into military or
naval service

stowaway
someone or something that hides
on a ship to travel in secret

subdue
to take command of an individual
or group by force

swag
stolen money or goods

INDEX